English
made easy

Key Stage 1
Ages 5-6

Author Brenda Apsley
Consultant Claire White

Certificate

Congratulations to ....
for successfully finishing this book.

☆ *You're a star!* ☆

Initial and final sounds

Write the letters of the **initial** sounds to finish these words.

Remember: The **initial** sound is the first sound in a word.

 __ater

 __all

 __oe

 __umb

Write the letters of the **final** sounds to finish these words.

Remember: The **final** sound is the last sound in a word.

 te__

 pea__

 gir__

 bir__

Now play the alphabet game. Say two words that start with **a**, such as **ant** and **as**. Next, say two words that start with **b**, then **c**. Say two words for each letter of the alphabet, ending with **z**.

2

Medial sounds a, e and i

Say these words with the **a** sound in the middle.

Remember: The **medial** letter is the middle letter in a word.

bat van

Write **a** words for these pictures.

....

Say these words with the **e** sound in the middle.

leg set

Choose a word from the box to finish the sentence below.

| ten   den   men |

Pen the hen has .... eggs.

Read out loud the words with **i** in the middle. Write them on Bill's big bin.

sat   put

sit   not

lot   lit

hit   set

tin   tip

....

....

....

Find the word that does not rhyme, and write it to finish the sentence below.

mat   win   pat   fat   cat

Lin wants to .... the race.

Medial sounds o and u

Read out loud the words with **o** in the middle. Write them on Pol's box.

get   got
hit   lot
pat   pin
mug   pot
not   dog

....

....

....

Find the word that does not rhyme, and write it to finish the sentence below.

tug   hug   lot   mug   rug

Jon has a .... of pens.

How many sounds can you say with the **u** sound in the middle, like in **hug**?

Write a **u** word for each picture.

....

Choose a word from the box to finish the sentence, then write the whole sentence.

rug mug tum

Ug the bug has a big ....

....

Compound words

Some words are made up of two other words. When two short words make one long word, the long word is called a **compound word**.

Try these word sums. Write the two words without a space between them to make one **compound word**, like this: **head** + **rest** = **headrest**.

lamp + post = lamppost ....

her + self = ...

milk + man = ...

hand + bag = ...

foot + stool = ...

Draw lines to join up these **compound words**.

foot   card   play   bag

him   cake   school   man

post   ball   post   spoon

pan   self   tea   ground

Now write a list of the **compound words** that you joined above.

....

....

....

....

The ai sound

Different letter sets can make the same sound. The letter sets **ai**, **a_e** and **ay** make the same sound. For example: s**ai**l s**ale** s**ay**

Write **ai** to spell these words. Read the words, then write them.
Draw lines to match two of the **ai** words to the pictures.

t__ __l ....

sn__ __l ....

tr__ __n ....

s__ __l ....

Write **a** and **e** to spell these words. Read the words, then write them.
Draw lines to match two of the **a_e** words to the pictures.

n__m__ ....

s__m__ ....

c__m__ ....

pl__t__ ....

Mary Dell

Write **ay** to spell these words. Read the words, then write them.
Draw lines to match two of the **ay** words to the pictures.

s__ __ ....

cl__ __ ....

d__ __ ....

tr__ __ ....

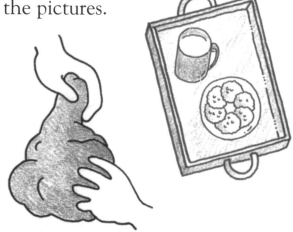

An action rhyme

Say the **rhyme** and do some actions to go with it.

Incy Wincy Spider

Incy Wincy spider
    climbed up the water spout,
Down came the raindrops
    and washed poor Incy out.
Out came the sunshine
    and dried up all the rain,
So Incy Wincy spider
    climbed up the spout again!

Draw Incy Wincy to finish the picture.

Write the words in the **rhyme** that have the **ai** spelling pattern.

....

The *ee* sound

Different letter sets can make the same sound. The letters **ee** and **ea** can make the same sound. The spelling is different but the sound is the same – b**ee**n sounds like b**ea**n. Read these **ee** words out loud.

feet   see   sheep   been   three
feel   sweet   seed   sleep   tree

Write **ee** words to match the pictures.

  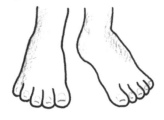

....

Now write these sentences.

Count sheep if you cannot sleep.
One, two, three.

....

....

Read these **ea** words out loud.

meat   neat   seat   seal   real
cream   team   bead   heat   bean

Write **ea** words to match these pictures.

....

The ie sound

Different letter sets make the same sound. The letter sets **ie, i_e, igh** and **y** sound the same.

Read the words in the big balloon. Then write the words in the small balloons.

nine
sigh   by
try   bite
my
tie
five   lie
high
dry
fly

ie words

....

....

i_e words

....

....

....

igh words

....

....

y words

....

....

....

....

....

Numbers 1 to 20

Read these **number words**. Write a **numeral** for each one.

one .... five .... eight ....
two .... six .... nine ....
three .... seven .... ten ....
four ....

Draw lines to match the **number words** to the **numerals**.

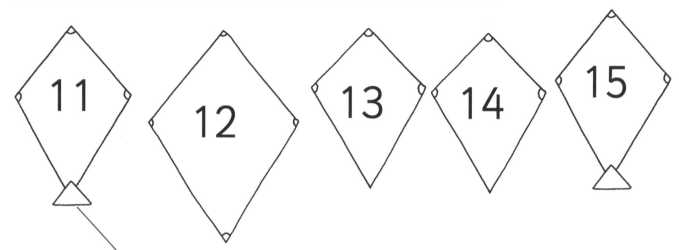

thirteen   eleven   twelve   fifteen   fourteen

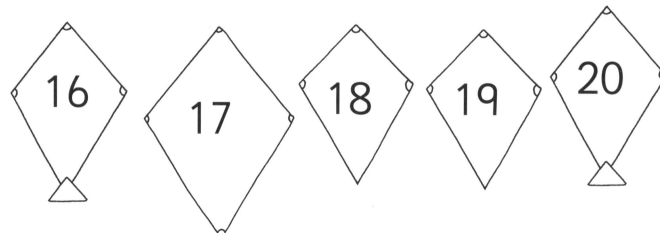

seventeen   sixteen   nineteen   twenty   eighteen

Vowels and consonants

Say the letters of the **alphabet** out loud or sing them.

a b c d e f g h i j k l m n o p q r s t u v w x y z

There are two kinds of letters.
These letters are **vowels**.
a e i o u y

These letters are **consonants**.

b c d f g h j k l m n p q r s t v w x y z

The letter **y** is special. It can be a **vowel** or a **consonant** depending on the sound it makes.

Look at the **first** letters in these words. Write **v** for **vowel** or **c** for **consonant** after each one.

the ☐   end ☐   in ☐   get ☐   up ☐

Look at the **middle** letters. Write **v** or **c** after each one.

big ☐   bus ☐   and ☐   you ☐   she ☐

Look at the **last** letters. Write **v** or **c** after each one.

see ☐   want ☐   with ☐   who ☐   new ☐

A fantasy story

Ask a grown-up to read this **story** to you. Then read it out loud yourself.

Whatever Next!
by Jill Murphy

"Can I go to the moon?" asked Baby Bear.
    "No, you can't," said Mrs Bear. "It's bathtime.
Anyway, you'd have to find a rocket first."
    Baby Bear found a rocket in the cupboard under the stairs.
He found a space-helmet on the draining board in the kitchen,
and a pair of space-boots on the mat by the front door.
He packed his teddy and some food for the journey and
took off up the chimney …
… WHOOSH! Out into the night.

Now tell the **story** in your own words.

What do you think Baby Bear used as
a rocket? Tick a picture.

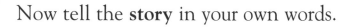
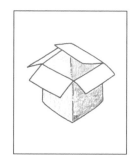

What did Baby Bear use as space-boots?
Tick a picture.

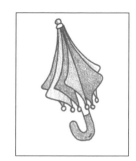

What was Baby Bear's space-helmet?
Tick a picture.

Draw pictures of things you would take to the moon.

The oo sound

Different letter sets make the same sound. The letters **oo** and **u_e** make the same sound. So do **ew** and **ue**. The spelling is different, but the sound is the same.

Read the words on the **moon**. Then sort the words into sets by writing them on the stars.

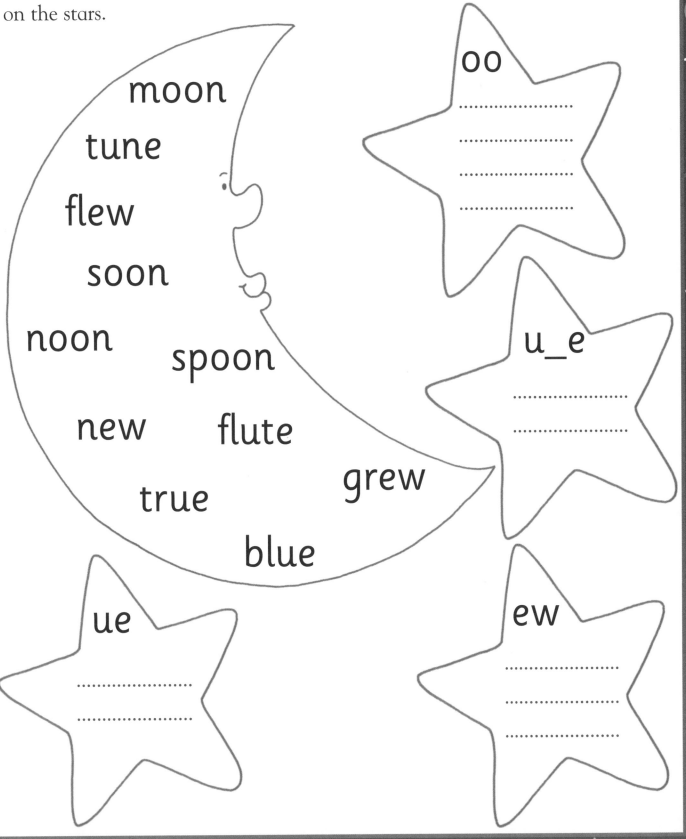

moon
tune
flew
soon
noon
spoon
new
flute
true
grew
blue

oo
....
....
....
....

u_e
....
....

ue
....
....

ew
....
....
....

Classroom words

Use the words below to write labels for this **classroom**.

map   desk   table   bin   fish

books   teacher   clock   chair   plant

Write about the things in your **classroom**.

....

....

The oa sound

Different letter sets make the same sound. The letter sets **oa**, **o_e** and **ow** make the same sound.

Read these words with the **oa** spelling. Draw the missing pictures.

boat	soap	coat

Draw rings around the words with the **o_e** spelling pattern.

pole   low   coal   hole   note   slow

Write **ow** to finish each word. Then write the whole word.

l__ __   ....

sn__ __   ....

wind__ __   ....

Write a **label** for the picture.

....

A poem to share

Read and learn this **poem**.

The More it Snows
by A. A. Milne

The more it
SNOWS-tiddely-pom,
The more it
GOES-tiddely-pom
The more it
GOES-tiddely-pom
On
Snowing.

And nobody
KNOWS-tiddely-pom,
How cold my
TOES-tiddely-pom
How cold my
TOES-tiddely-pom
Are
Growing.

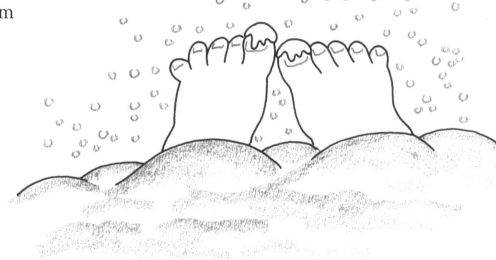

You learned about the **oa** sound on page 15. Now write down all the **oa** sound words in the poem.

Remember: The letter sets **oa**, **o_e** and **ow** all make the **oa** sound.

....

....

Verbs

A **verb** is a doing or being word. Read these words. They are all **verbs**.

move   jump   cry   help   pull   push

Which of the following words are **verbs**? Write them down.

jump   she   then   more   dig   he
hop   run   here   play   but   lie

....

....

Write **verbs** to finish these sentences. Use **verbs** from the list you made above.

Things I do

First I .... with my dog.

I .... as fast as I can.

I .... over the wall.

Then I .... on one leg.

Next I .... in the sand.

After all that I .... down.

Verb tenses

A **verb** is a word that tells you what something or somebody is doing or being.

Different **verb** endings tell us **when** things happen.

Verbs ending in **-ing** tell us that something is happening **now**.

Verbs ending in **-ed** tell us that something happened before.

Read these sentences. Write **-ing** or **-ed** to finish the **verbs**.

I am play............... with my cat today.

Last night I help........... my mum.

This morning I jump......... in a puddle.

Jo is push........ the truck, Kim is pull........ it.

It rain........... yesterday.

18

Weather words

The pictures show what the **weather** is like each day.
Draw lines to match the **weather words** to the pictures.

rain    sun

snow    fog

wind   cloud

Write a **weather word** for each picture.

....

Use these sentences to help you write about **weather**. Write in the missing
days of the week, and draw the missing pictures.

Monday was warm and cloudy.
It was very cold on Wednesday.
We got wet on Thursday.

Monday   ....   Wednesday

Thursday   ....

Themed rhymes

Do you say these **rhymes** at school?

It's raining, it's pouring,
The old man is snoring.
He went to bed
And bumped his head,
And couldn't get up in the morning.

Rain, rain, go away,
Come again another day.

Rain on the green grass,
And rain on the tree.
Rain on the house top,
But not on me.

Write words that **rhyme** with these words. You can find them in the **rhymes**.

day ....   pouring ....

me ....   bed ....

Now read this **poem**.

Rain

by Spike Milligan

There are holes in the sky
Where the rain gets in,
But they're ever so small
That's why rain is thin.

Do you like this **poem**? Say why.

Try writing your own poem about the weather.

Punctuation

Every sentence begins with a capital letter.
We use a **question mark** at the end of a sentence that asks a question.
The **question mark** takes the place of a **full stop**.

Write a **full stop** or a **question mark** at the end of each sentence below.
Then write the whole sentence, starting with a capital letter.

do you like dogs   ....

i like dogs a lot   ....

i like cats as well   ....

do you like them   ....

do you have a pet   ....

what is your pet's name   ....

my pet is called Kit   ....

i love my pet   ....

We use an **exclamation mark** at the end of a sentence that shows
surprise or gives a command.

Write an **exclamation mark** in the spaces below.

The policeman said, "Stop ...."

The swimmer called, "Help ...."

The climber shouted, "Look out ...."

The patient cried, "Ouch ...."

Recording information

Write about yourself. First draw a picture. Then write your **name**.

Remember: Names of people and places start with a **capital letter**. **Sentences** end with a **full stop**.

My name is ....

Write your **age**.

I am .... years old.

Where do you **live**? Draw a picture of your home. Put a number on the door.

Write your address.

I live at ....

Read these **doing words**: read   write   spell

Write the words to make **sentences** about yourself.

I can ....

I can ....

I can ....

Sequencing a story

Look at the pictures. Put them in the right order. Write the numbers in the red boxes. Tell the story in your own words.

The Tortoise and the Hare

Themed poems

These **poems** are about food.

When Susie's Eating Custard
by John Foster

When Susie's eating custard,
She gets it everywhere.
Down her bib, up her nose,
All over her high chair.

She pokes it with her fingers.
She spreads it on her hair.
When Susie's eating custard,
She gets it everywhere.

Draw Susie in her high chair.

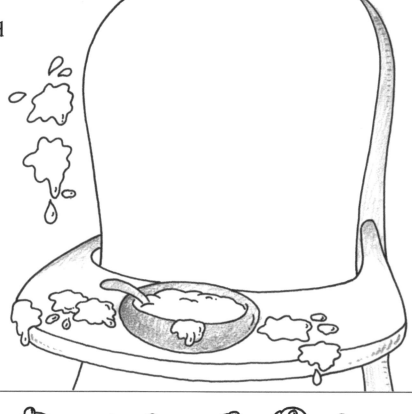

I scream, you scream
We all scream for ice cream!

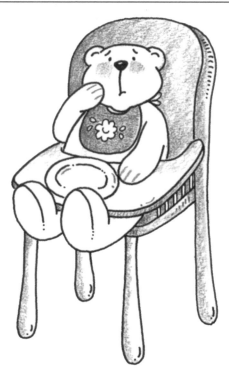

Teddy Bear
by L. H. Allen

Teddy Bear
Sat on a chair,
With ham and jam
And plum and pear.

"This is queer,"
Said Teddy Bear,
"The more I eat
The less is there!"

Talk about the **poems**. Which one do you like best? Say why.

Contents and index

You can use **information books** to find out about things.
Information books are **non-fiction**.
This one is about pets.

The list at the front is called the **contents** list.
It tells you the main things that are in the book
and on what pages you can find them.

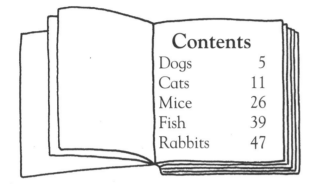

Write the **page numbers** for these pets.

Mice ....

Dogs ....

Fish ....

The list at the back of the book is called the **index**.
It is a list of all the things in the book and their **page numbers**.

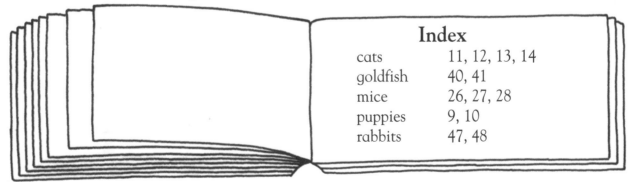

Which pages are about goldfish? ....

Can you read about cats on page 40? ....

Is the **index** in **alphabetical order**? ....

Dictionaries

A **dictionary** is a book of words.
It helps you **spell** words.
It tells you what words **mean**.
Some **dictionaries** have pictures.
Some do not have pictures.

The words in a **dictionary** are in **alphabetical order**.
Words beginning with **a** are at the **front** of a **dictionary**.
Words beginning with **z** are at the **back** of a **dictionary**.

pP
pet: a pet is an animal that lives with us.

Here are some words from a **dictionary**.

<table>
<tr><td>train</td><td>ride</td><td>park</td><td>enjoy</td><td>dream</td></tr>
<tr><td>bread</td><td>winter</td><td>shirt</td><td>zoo</td><td>coat</td></tr>
</table>

Which word is nearest the front?   ....

Which is nearest the back?   ....

Write a list of **animal words** in the order that they come in the **dictionary**.
Use the animals in these pictures.

....

....

....

....

A fantasy story

Read this **story** in a spooky voice.

In a dark, dark wood
was a dark, dark house.

In the dark, dark house
was a dark, dark room.

In the dark, dark room
was a dark, dark chest.

In the dark, dark chest
was a dark, dark box.

In the dark, dark box
was a …

What do you think was in the dark, dark box? Draw a picture of it.

Write a **title** for this story.

Remember: The **title** is the name of the story. The words in a **title** start with **capital letters**.

....

Read the **story** again. Say something different is in the dark, dark box this time.

Fiction and non-fiction

We call books that are made up **fiction**. The stories are not real.

We call books that are true **non-fiction**. The things in them are real.

Book **covers** help us sort **fiction** and **non-fiction** books.
The **title** helps. So does the **picture**.

Write the **titles** of these books on the correct lists below.

fiction   non-fiction

....

....

28

Non-fiction

Information books tell us things. They are **non-fiction**.
We use **information books** to find out about real things.

Which books tell us about which things? Draw lines to match them.

Farm Animals

My First Atlas

Things That Go

What does this book tell us about?
Draw a picture on the cover.

Trees

Some **information books** tell us about lots of different things. To make the things easier to find, they are in **alphabetical order**. Things that start with a are near the **front**. Things that start with z are near the **back**.

Draw lines to match the pictures below to the words from the information book.

| a | d | s |
| ant | dog | sun |

Question words

We ask **questions** when we want to find out things. Write these words that ask **questions**. Which is the odd one out? Say why.

who   what   why   when   where   how

....

Write a **question** word and add a **question mark** to finish each sentence.

Remember: Sentences that ask **questions** have a **question mark** at the end.

.... has been sitting in my chair

.... do you live

I am six. .... old are you

.... does lunch time start

.... do you like this book

Hello, ... is your name

Recounting events

Write about a day at your school. The words on the **poster** will help you. Look up any words you need in a **word book** or **dictionary**. D

Remember: The words in a **dictionary** are in **alphabetical order**.

First we ....

Next we ....

Then we ....

After lunch we...................................

Last of all we.....................................

read	home
go	sing
spell	paint
sums	write
play	bake

Draw a picture of something you do at school.

The days of the week

There are seven days in a **week**. Each day has its own **name**.
Read and write the days of the **week**.

Remember: Names of the days of the week start with a **capital letter.**

Sunday	....	
Monday	....	
Tuesday	....	
Wednesday	....	
Thursday	....	
Friday	....	
Saturday	....	

On which days do you go to school? Say the **names**.

On which days do you stay at home? Write the **names**.

.... and ....

What day is it today? Write a **sentence**.

Today is ....

Answer Section with Parents' Notes

Key Stage 1
Ages 5–6

This 8-page section provides answers or explanatory notes to all the activities in this book. This will enable you to assess your child's work.

Work through each page together, and ensure that your child understands each task. Point out any mistakes, and correct any handwriting errors. (Your child should use the handwriting style taught at his or her school.) As well as making corrections, it is very important to praise your child's efforts and achievements.

Encourage your child to develop the habit of using a word book or dictionary to find the meaning and correct spelling of a new word.

---

2 ⭐ Initial and final sounds

Write the letters of the **initial** sounds to finish these words.
Remember: The **initial** sound is the first sound in a word.

w ater   b all
sh oe   th umb

Write the letters of the **final** sounds to finish these words.
Remember: The **final** sound is the last sound in a word.

te n   pea ch
gir l   bir d

Now play the alphabet game. Say two words that start with **a**, such as **ant** and **as**. Next, say two words that start with **b**, then **c**. Say two words for each letter of the alphabet, ending with **z**.

This page builds on your child's work on initial and final letter sounds. He or she should become familiar with the meanings of the terms *initial* (first) and *final* (last). Explain the words and discuss them together if necessary.

---

3 Medial sounds a, e and i ⭐

Say these words with the **a** sound in the middle.
Remember: The **medial** letter is the middle letter in a word.

bat van

Write **a** words for these pictures.

fan   cap   jam

Say these words with the **e** sound in the middle.

leg set

Choose a word from the box to finish the sentence below.

| ten den men |

Pen the hen has ...... ten ...... eggs.

Read out loud the words with **i** in the middle. Write them on Bill's big bin.

sat   put
sit   not
lot   lit
hit   set
tin   tip

sit   tin
lit   tip
hit

Find the word that does not rhyme, and write it to finish the sentence below.

mat   win   pat   fat   cat

Lin wants to ...... win ...... the race.

Your child needs to understand the word *medial* (middle). Encourage him or her to say the *a, e* and *i* sounds out loud and to combine them with initial and final consonants to read, spell and write common CVC (consonant vowel consonant) words.

---

4 ⭐ Medial sounds o and u

Read out loud the words with **o** in the middle. Write them on Pol's box.

get   got
hit   lot
pat   pin
mug   pot
not   dog

got   not
lot   dog
pot

Find the word that does not rhyme, and write it to finish the sentence below.

tug   hug   lot   mug   rug

Jon has a ...... lot ...... of pens.

How many sounds can you say with the **u** sound in the middle, like in **hug**?
Write a **u** word for each picture.

jug   bun   cup

Choose a word from the box to finish the sentence, then write the whole sentence.

| rug mug tum |

Ug the bug has a big ...... mug ......
Ug the bug has a big mug.

This page focuses on the *medial* (middle) sounds *o* and *u*. Your child should say the vowel sounds out loud, then combine them with initial and final consonant sounds in CVC words. Saying words out loud will help your child identify difficult sounds.

Compound words

Some words are made up of two other words. When two short words make one long word, the long word is called a **compound word**.

Try these word sums. Write the two words without a space between them to make one **compound word**, like this: head + rest = headrest.

lamp + post = lamppost
her + self = herself
milk + man = milkman
hand + bag = handbag
foot + stool = footstool

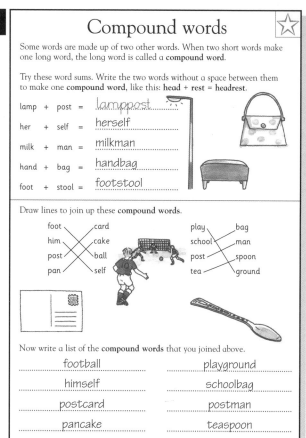

Draw lines to join up these **compound words**.

foot — card
him — cake
post — ball
pan — self

play — bag
school — man
post — spoon
tea — ground

Now write a list of the **compound words** that you joined above.

football   playground
himself   schoolbag
postcard   postman
pancake   teaspoon

Help your child learn to split familiar compound words into their component parts, for example, *football* is made up of *foot* and *ball*. He or she may find it helpful to think of compound words and their component parts as simple sums.

The ai sound

Different letter sets can make the same sound. The letter sets **ai**, **a_e** and **ay** make the same sound. For example: **sail sale say**

Write **ai** to spell these words. Read the words, then write them. Draw lines to match two of the **ai** words to the pictures.

t_a__i_l   tail
sn_a__i_l   snail
tr_a__i_n   train
s_a_il   sail

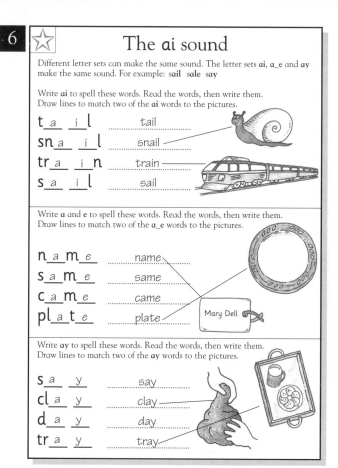

Write **a** and **e** to spell these words. Read the words, then write them. Draw lines to match two of the **a_e** words to the pictures.

n_a_m_e_   name
s_a_m_e_   same
c_a_m_e_   came
pl_a_t_e_   plate

Mary Dell

Write **ay** to spell these words. Read the words, then write them. Draw lines to match two of the **ay** words to the pictures.

s_a__y   say
cl_a__y   clay
d_a__y   day
tr_a__y   tray

Some children find it confusing that different letter sets, or groups of letters, can make the same sound. Help your child by looking at this page together, building familiarity through repeating sounds, saying words aloud and writing the letters.

An action rhyme

Say the **rhyme** and do some actions to go with it.

Incy Wincy Spider

Incy Wincy spider
   climbed up the water spout,
Down came the raindrops
   and washed poor Incy out.
Out came the sunshine
   and dried up all the rain,
So Incy Wincy spider
   climbed up the spout again!

Draw Incy Wincy to finish the picture.

Write the words in the **rhyme** that have the **ai** spelling pattern.

raindrops   rain   again

Action rhymes make learning fun. Your child should use his or her hands to make a spider that climbs up and down. He or she will soon learn the rhyme by heart. Help your child find and write the *ai* words *rain* and *again*.

The ee sound

Different letter sets can make the same sound. The letters **ee** and **ea** can make the same sound. The spelling is different but the sound is the same – **been** sounds like **bean**. Read these **ee** words out loud.

feet   see   sheep   been   three
feel   sweet   seed   sleep   tree

Write **ee** words to match the pictures.

sweet   sheep   feet

Now write these sentences.

**Count sheep if you cannot sleep.
One, two, three.**

Count sheep if you cannot sleep.
One, two, three.

Read these **ea** words out loud.

meat   neat   seat   seal   real
cream   team   bead   heat   bean

Write **ea** words to match these pictures.

seat   bean   seal

These letter sets or groups make the same *ee* sound. Help by explaining that words that sound the same, such as *see* and *sea*, can be spelled differently. With lots of exposure to such words, children will soon learn the different spellings.

The ie sound ☆

Different letter sets make the same sound. The letter sets **ie**, **i_e**, **igh** and **y** sound the same.

Read the words in the big balloon. Then write the words in the small balloons.

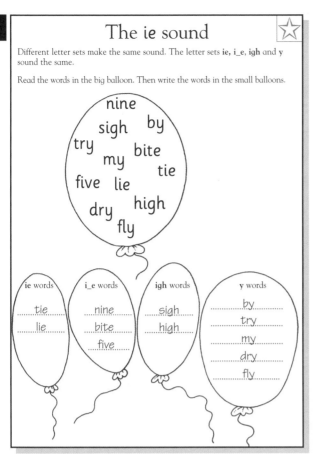

nine
sigh by
try bite
my
tie
five lie
high
dry
fly

ie words	**i_e** words	**igh** words	**y** words
tie	nine	sigh	by
lie	bite	high	try
	five		my
			dry
			fly

Four letter sets make the same *ie* sound as in *tie*. Build confidence in reading and spelling these words by introducing your child to the variety of forms. Saying the words out loud will emphasise the different spelling pattern rules.

☆ Numbers 1 to 20

Read these **number words**. Write a **numeral** for each one.

one	1	five	5	eight	8
two	2	six	6	nine	9
three	3	seven	7	ten	10
four	4				

Draw lines to match the **number words** to the **numerals**.

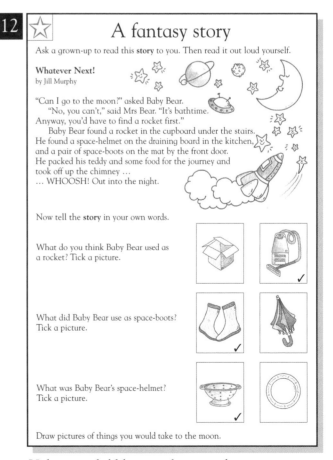

11   12   13   14   15

thirteen   eleven   twelve   fifteen   fourteen

16   17   18   19   20

seventeen   sixteen   nineteen   twenty   eighteen

It is important that your child makes the link between numerals (1, 2, 3, etc.) and number words and is able to use both with confidence. Encourage him or her to identify number words with spelling patterns such as adding the suffix *-teen*.

Vowels and consonants ☆

Say the letters of the **alphabet** out loud or sing them.

a b c d e f g h i j k l m n o p q r s t u v w x y z

There are two kinds of letters.
These letters are **vowels**.
a e i o u y

These letters are **consonants**.
b c d f g h j k l m n p q r s t v w x y z

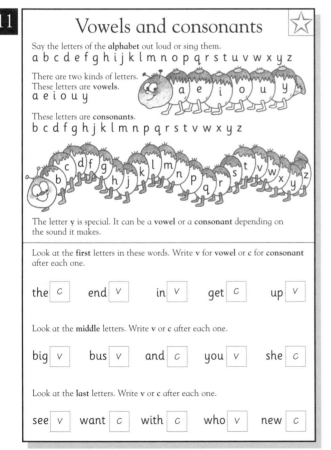

The letter **y** is special. It can be a **vowel** or a **consonant** depending on the sound it makes.

Look at the **first** letters in these words. Write **v** for **vowel** or **c** for **consonant** after each one.

the c   end v   in v   get c   up v

Look at the **middle** letters. Write **v** or **c** after each one.

big v   bus v   and c   you v   she c

Look at the **last** letters. Write **v** or **c** after each one.

see v   want c   with c   who v   new c

Your child should know the letters of the alphabet and be able to sing or say them in order. He or she should also become familiar with vowels (*a, e, i, o, u and y*) and consonants. Explain that y can be a vowel or a consonant depending on its sound.

☆ A fantasy story

Ask a grown-up to read this **story** to you. Then read it out loud yourself.

Whatever Next!
by Jill Murphy

"Can I go to the moon?" asked Baby Bear.
"No, you can't," said Mrs Bear. "It's bathtime. Anyway, you'd have to find a rocket first."
Baby Bear found a rocket in the cupboard under the stairs. He found a space-helmet on the draining board in the kitchen, and a pair of space-boots on the mat by the front door. He packed his teddy and some food for the journey and took off up the chimney …
… WHOOSH! Out into the night.

Now tell the **story** in your own words.

What do you think Baby Bear used as a rocket? Tick a picture.

What did Baby Bear use as space-boots? Tick a picture.

What was Baby Bear's space-helmet? Tick a picture.

Draw pictures of things you would take to the moon.

Help your child learn to listen and concentrate as you read the story out loud, then retell it in his or her own words. Re-read the story if necessary. The activities on this page test your child's comprehension and understanding of the story.

The oo sound

Different letter sets make the same sound. The letters **oo** and **u_e** make the same sound. So do **ew** and **ue**. The spelling is different, but the sound is the same.

Read the words on the **moon**. Then sort the words into sets by writing them on the stars.

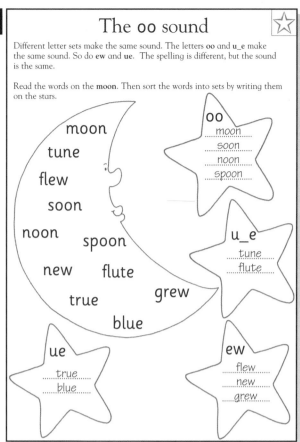

moon
tune
flew
soon
noon   spoon
new   flute
true   grew
blue
ue
true
blue

oo
moon
soon
noon
spoon

u_e
tune
flute

ew
flew
new
grew

Four letter sets make the same *oo* sound as in *moon*. Saying the words out loud will help your child associate the sound with the different spelling patterns. Sorting into sets makes a game of the activity and is useful handwriting practice.

Classroom words

Use the words below to write labels for this **classroom**.

map   desk   table   bin   fish
books   teacher   clock · chair   plant

map
clock
books
bin
fish
desk
plant
teacher
chair
table

Write about the things in your **classroom**.

Answers may vary

Your child will be very familiar with his or her own school classroom. Encourage him or her to compare it with the classroom in the illustration and help him or her choose and write labels. Offer help with spelling if it is required.

The oa sound

Different letter sets make the same sound. The letter sets **oa**, **o_e** and **ow** make the same sound.

Read these words with the **oa** spelling. Draw the missing pictures.

boat   soap   coat

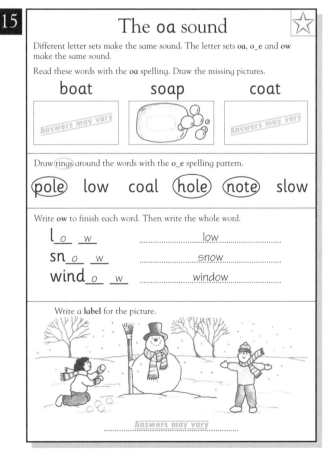

Answers may vary   *Answers may vary*

Draw rings around the words with the o_e spelling pattern.

(pole)   low   coal   (hole)   (note)   slow

Write **ow** to finish each word. Then write the whole word.

l o w   low
sn o w   snow
wind o w   window

Write a **label** for the picture.

Answers may vary

These activities will help your child read and spell more same sound, different spelling words, this time the *oa* sound as in *boat*. Talk about the snow picture, and help your child write words, a phrase or a sentence, depending upon ability level.

A poem to share

Read and learn this **poem**.

The More it Snows
by A. A. Milne

The more it
SNOWS-tiddely-pom,
The more it
GOES-tiddely-pom
The more it
GOES-tiddely-pom
On
Snowing.

And nobody
KNOWS-tiddely-pom,
How cold my
TOES-tiddely-pom
How cold my
TOES-tiddely-pom
Are
Growing.

You learned about the **oa** sound on page 15. Now write down all the **oa** sound words in the poem.

Remember: The letter sets **oa**, **o_e** and **ow** all make the **oa** sound.

snows   goes   snowing   knows   toes   growing

Read the poem with your child, pointing to the words and placing emphasis on those in capital letters. Repeat it to help your child learn it by heart, pausing to allow him or her to contribute key words. Help him or her identify *oa* sound words.

Verbs ☆

A **verb** is a doing or being word. Read these words. They are all **verbs**.

move   jump   cry   help   pull   push

Which of the following words are **verbs**? Write them down.

jump   she   then   more   dig   he
hop   run   here   play   but   lie

...... jump .... hop .... play ......
...... dig .... run ......

Write **verbs** to finish these sentences. Use **verbs** from the list you made above.

Things I do

First I ...... play ...... with my dog.

I ...... run ...... as fast as I can.

I ...... jump ...... over the wall.

Then I ...... hop ...... on one leg.

Next I ...... dig ...... in the sand.

After all that I ...... lie ...... down.

This page introduces verbs: "doing" and "being" words, such as *spell*, *jump* and *cry*. Talk about verbs with your child, giving lots of examples. Help him or her select and make a list of verbs and write them to complete the sentences.

Verb tenses

A **verb** is a word that tells you what something or somebody is doing or being.
Different **verb** endings tell us **when** things happen.
Verbs ending in -**ing** tell us that something is happening **now**.
Verbs ending in -**ed** tell us that something happened before.

Read these sentences. Write -**ing** or -**ed** to finish the **verbs**.

I am play ...ing... with my cat today.

Last night I help ...ed... my mum.

This morning I jump ...ed... in a puddle.

Jo is push ...ing... the truck, Kim is pull ...ing... it.

It rain ...ed... yesterday.

This page consolidates the verb activities on page 17 and expands the concept, introducing tenses (verb endings). Talk about the different meanings of verbs that end -*ing* (present tense) and -*ed* (past tense). Help your child make selections.

Weather words ☆

The pictures show what the **weather** is like each day. Draw lines to match the **weather words** to the pictures.

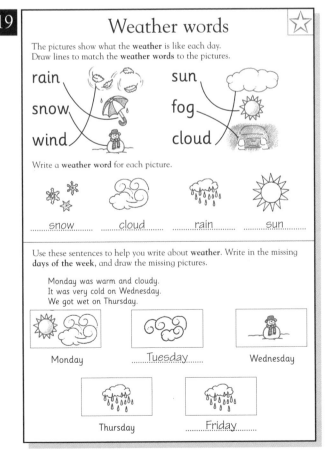

rain   sun
snow   fog
wind   cloud

Write a **weather word** for each picture.

...... snow .... cloud .... rain .... sun ......

Use these sentences to help you write about **weather**. Write in the missing **days of the week**, and draw the missing pictures.

Monday was warm and cloudy.
It was very cold on Wednesday.
We got wet on Thursday.

Monday   Tuesday   Wednesday

Thursday   Friday

Many school classrooms have a weather chart. Your child should be able to read and write familiar weather words. Talk about weather and encourage your child to make use of the written information on the page.

Themed rhymes

Do you say these **rhymes** at school?

It's raining, it's pouring,
The old man is snoring.
He went to bed
And bumped his head,
And couldn't get up in the morning.

Rain, rain, go away,
Come again another day.

Rain on the green grass,
And rain on the tree.
Rain on the house top,
But not on me.

Write words that **rhyme** with these words. You can find them in the **rhymes**.

day ...... away ......   pouring ...... snoring ......

me ...... tree ......   bed ...... head ......

Now read this **poem**.

Rain
by Spike Milligan

There are holes in the sky
Where the rain gets in,
But they're ever so small
That's why rain is thin.

Do you like this **poem**? Say why.

Try writing your own poem about the weather.

Read the poems about rain to your child in a lively, sing-song style, then encourage him or her to join in. Talk about similarities, differences and preferences together. Help your child to re-read the poems carefully to find the rhyming words.

Punctuation

Every sentence begins with a capital letter.
We use a **question mark** at the end of a sentence that asks a question.
The **question mark** takes the place of a **full stop**.

Write a **full stop** or a **question mark** at the end of each sentence below.
Then write the whole sentence, starting with a capital letter.

do you like dogs	Do you like dogs?
i like dogs a lot	I like dogs a lot.
i like cats as well	I like cats as well.
do you like them	Do you like them?
do you have a pet	Do you have a pet?
what is your pet's name	What is your pet's name?
my pet is called Kit	My pet is called Kit.
i love my pet	I love my pet.

We use an **exclamation mark** at the end of a sentence that shows surprise or gives a command.

Write an **exclamation mark** in the spaces below.

The policeman said, "Stop ___!___ "

The swimmer called, "Help ___!___ "

The climber shouted, "Look out ___!___ "

The patient cried, "Ouch ___!___ "

Punctuation helps reading and writing accuracy. Explain that punctuation marks help us make sense of text and how a question mark indicates a question. It will help if you say each sentence as a flat statement and then as a question.

Recording information

Write about yourself. First draw a picture.
Then write your **name**.

Remember: Names of people and places start with a **capital letter**. Sentences end with a **full stop**.

My name is............*Answers may vary*............

Write your **age**.

I am .... years old.

Where do you **live**?
Draw a picture of your home.
Put a number on the door.

Write your address.

I live at ....*Answers may vary*............

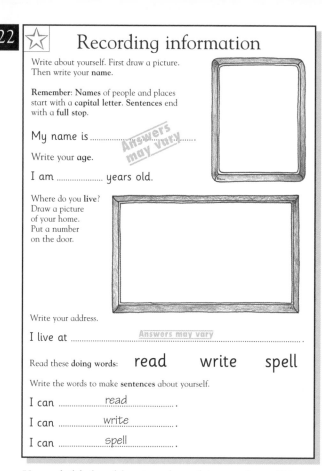

Read these **doing words**: **read   write   spell**

Write the words to make **sentences** about yourself.

I can ....read............ .

I can ....write............ .

I can ....spell............ .

Your child should write about him- or herself in sentences. This page also records the skills your child has developed in this book. Continue to be lavish with your praise for work well done.

Sequencing a story

Look at the pictures. Put them in the right order. Write the numbers in the red boxes. Tell the story in your own words.

The Tortoise and the Hare

This page focuses on the difference between the beginning, middle and end of a story. Make sure your child has the sequence correct and then ask him or her to describe what is going on in each picture, including dialogue and thoughts of the characters.

Themed poems

These **poems** are about food.

When Susie's Eating Custard
by John Foster

When Susie's eating custard,
She gets it everywhere.
Down her bib, up her nose,
All over her high chair.

She pokes it with her fingers.
She spreads it on her hair.
When Susie's eating custard,
She gets it everywhere.

Draw Susie in her high chair.

I scream, you scream
We all scream for ice cream!

Teddy Bear
by L. H. Allen

Teddy Bear
Sat on a chair,
With ham and jam
And plum and pear.

"This is queer,"
Said Teddy Bear,
"The more I eat
The less is there!"

Talk about the **poems**. Which one do you like best? Say why.

This page has a collection of poems with a food theme. Read the poems out loud, then say them together. Listen as your child reads or recites. Talk about the word *poem* and what it means and point out the poets' names.

Contents and index

You can use **information books** to find out about things.
Information books are **non-fiction**.
This one is about pets.

The list at the front is called the **contents** list.
It tells you the main things that are in the book
and on what pages you can find them.

Contents	
Dogs	5
Cats	11
Mice	26
Fish	39
Rabbits	47

Write the **page numbers** for these pets.

Mice .....26.....

Dogs .....5.....

Fish .....39.....

The list at the back of the book is called the **index**.
It is a list of all the things in the book and their **page numbers**.

Index	
cats	11, 12, 13, 14
goldfish	40, 41
mice	26, 27, 28
puppies	9, 10
rabbits	47, 48

Which pages are about goldfish? .....40, 41.....

Can you read about cats on page 40? .....no.....

Is the **index** in **alphabetical order**? .....yes.....

Your child needs to understand the role of the
contents list and the index in non-fiction books.
Discuss how they can be used to source
information. You can extend the activity by
exploring a range of non-fiction books together.

Dictionaries

A **dictionary** is a book of words.
It helps you **spell** words.
It tells you what words **mean**.
Some **dictionaries** have pictures.
Some do not have pictures.

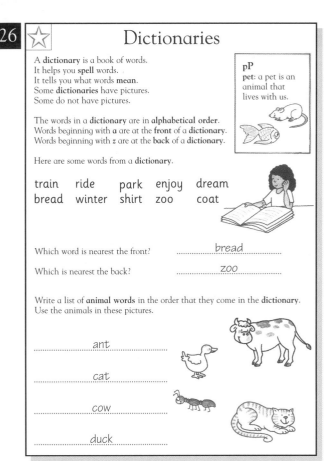

pP
pet: a pet is an animal that lives with us.

The words in a **dictionary** are in **alphabetical order**.
Words beginning with **a** are at the **front** of a **dictionary**.
Words beginning with **z** are at the **back** of a **dictionary**.

Here are some words from a **dictionary**.

| train | ride | park | enjoy | dream |
| bread | winter | shirt | zoo | coat |

Which word is nearest the front? .....bread.....

Which is nearest the back? .....zoo.....

Write a list of **animal words** in the order that they come in the **dictionary**.
Use the animals in these pictures.

.....ant.....

.....cat.....

.....cow.....

.....duck.....

A dictionary or word book is a very useful tool to
help your child spell, check spelling and find the
meanings of unfamiliar words. These activities
will help him or her explore and understand how
dictionaries work and how they are used.

A fantasy story

Read this **story** in a spooky voice.

In a dark, dark wood
was a dark, dark house.

In the dark, dark house
was a dark, dark room.

In the dark, dark room
was a dark, dark chest.

In the dark, dark chest
was a dark, dark box.

In the dark, dark box
was a ...

What do you think was in the dark, dark box? Draw a picture of it.

Write a **title** for this story.

Remember: The **title** is the name of the story. The words in a **title** start with **capital letters**.

..... Answers may vary .....

Read the **story** again. Say something different is in the dark, dark box this time.

Confident readers will be able to read the story
alone, but others may need help. Make a game
of the activity, waiting for your child to supply
punchlines, and encouraging him or her to use
imagination when drawing a spooky picture.

Fiction and non-fiction

We call books that are made up **fiction**. The stories are not real.

We call books that are true **non-fiction**. The things in them are real.

Book **covers** help us sort **fiction** and **non-fiction** books.
The **title** helps. So does the **picture**.

Write the **titles** of these books on the correct lists below.

fiction	non-fiction
Puss in Boots	How Cars Work
The Three Bears	Your Body

Your child needs to know the difference between
fiction and non-fiction. Talk about the two kinds
of text and how titles and pictures on book covers
can help differentiate between the two forms.
Sort through a selection of books with your child.

Non-fiction

Information books tell us things. They are **non-fiction**.
We use **information books** to find out about real things.

Which books tell us about which things? Draw lines to match them.

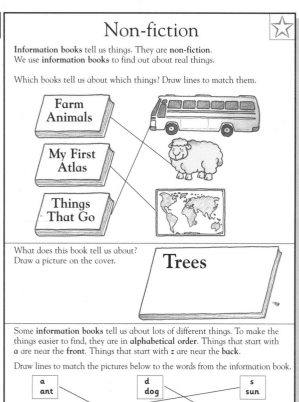

Farm Animals

My First Atlas

Things That Go

What does this book tell us about?
Draw a picture on the cover.

Trees

Some **information books** tell us about lots of different things. To make the things easier to find, they are in **alphabetical order**. Things that start with a are near the **front**. Things that start with z are near the **back**.

Draw lines to match the pictures below to the words from the information book.

| a ant | d dog | s sun |

Your child will see and use a wide range of non-fiction books at school. He or she should understand that text is often presented in alphabetical order and learn how to find information by looking under the subject's initial letter.

Question words

We ask **questions** when we want to find out things. Write these words that ask **questions**. Which is the odd one out? Say why.

who   what   why   when   where   how

who   what   why   when   where   how

Write a **question** word and add a **question mark** to finish each sentence.

Remember: Sentences that ask **questions** have a **question mark** at the end.

.......Who....... has been sitting in my chair?

.....Where..... do you live?

I am six. ......How...... old are you?

.....When..... does lunch time start?

.....Why..... do you like this book?

Hello, ...what...... is your name?

This page focuses on the use of question words and question marks. Help your child to select the odd question word (*how*: the only question word that does not begin with *wh-*) and to read and complete each sentence.

Recounting events

Write about a day at your school. The words on the **poster** will help you. Look up any words you need in a **word book** or **dictionary**. D

Remember: The words in a **dictionary** are in **alphabetical order**.

First we ...... Answers may vary

Next we ...... Answers may vary

Then we ...... Answers may vary

After lunch we ...... Answers may vary

Last of all we ...... Answers may vary

read	home
go	sing
spell	paint
sums	write
play	bake

Draw a picture of something you do at school.

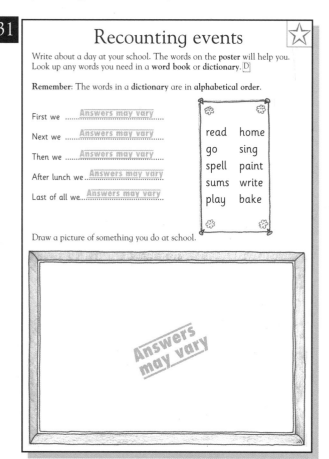

Answers may vary

Your child should learn how to record and recount events, understand the use of sequencing words such as *first* and *last*, and relate events to personal experience. Help your child use a word book or dictionary and explain how alphabetical order works.

The days of the week

There are seven days in a **week**. Each day has its own **name**.
Read and write the days of the **week**.

Remember: Names of the days of the week start with a **capital letter**.

Sunday	..........Sunday..........	
Monday	..........Monday..........	
Tuesday	Tuesday	
Wednesday	Wednesday	
Thursday	Thursday	
Friday	Friday	
Saturday	Saturday	

On which days do you go to school? Say the **names**.

On which days do you stay at home? Write the **names**.

........Saturday........ and ....Sunday........

What day is it today? Write a **sentence**.

Today is .... Answers may vary

Your child should be able to name, read and write the names of the days of the week. The questions prompt him or her to differentiate between week- and weekend days. Help with the final activity by looking at a calendar, newspaper or diary together.